~ Native American Lives ~

George Morrison
Modern Artist

Written by Staci Drouillard
Illustrated by Tashia Hart

Minnesota Humanities Center

Lerner Publications ◆ Minneapolis

GENEROUSLY SUPPORTED BY

This book has been supported by the Minnesota Humanities Center, generously funded through the Shakopee Mdewakanton Sioux Community (SMSC) through its Understand Native Minnesota campaign, also funded in part by the Arts and Cultural Heritage Fund that was created with the vote of the people of Minnesota on November 4, 2008, and the National Endowment for the Humanities.

Copyright © 2026 Minnesota Humanities Center

All rights reserved. International copyright secured. No part of this book may be reproduced, stored in a retrieval system, or transmitted in any form or by any means—electronic, mechanical, photocopying, recording, or otherwise—without the prior written permission of Lerner Publishing Group, Inc., except for the inclusion of brief quotations in an acknowledged review.

Lerner Publications Company
An imprint of Lerner Publishing Group, Inc.
241 First Avenue North
Minneapolis, MN 55401 USA

For reading levels and more information, look up this title at www.lernerbooks.com.

Illustration credits: Tashia Hart
Additional image credits: Joe McLeister/Star Tribune via Getty Images, back cover, p. 6; Cook County Historical Society, p. 18; © George Morrison Estate, courtesy Minneapolis Institute of Arts, p. 23; Victor Bloomfield, Minnesota Historical Society, p. 34; © George Morrison Estate, courtesy Bockley Gallery, p. 37; © George Morrison Estate, courtesy Minnesota Historical Society, p. 38. Background pattern: Anastasiia Gevko/Shutterstock.

Main body text set in Noto Serif. Typeface provided by Google Open Source.

Library of Congress Cataloging-in-Publication Data

Names: Drouillard, Staci Lola, author. | Hart, Tashia, illustrator.
Title: George Morrison : modern artist / written by Staci Drouillard ; illustrated by Tashia Hart.
Description: Minneapolis : Lerner Publications, [2026] | Series: Native American lives | Includes bibliographical references and index. | Audience: Ages 9–14 | Audience: Grades 4–6 | Summary: "George Morrison was a talented modernist artist from Minnesota. Learn all about Morrison's life, including his upbringing, the kinds of mediums he worked with, and his journey as an Ojibwe artist"— Provided by publisher.
Identifiers: LCCN 2025004057 (print) | LCCN 2025004058 (ebook) | ISBN 9798765671832 (paperback) | ISBN 9798765697382 (epub)
Subjects: LCSH: Morrison, George, 1919–2000—Juvenile literature. | Artists—United States—Biography—Juvenile literature. | Ojibwe artists—United States—Biography—Juvenile literature. | Modernism (Art)—United States—Juvenile literature.
Classification: LCC N6537.M656 D76 2026 (print) | LCC N6537.M656 (ebook) | DDC 759.13—dc23/eng/20250429

LC record available at https://lccn.loc.gov/2025004057
LC ebook record available at https://lccn.loc.gov/2025004058

Manufactured in the United States of America
1-1012551-54285-4/25/2025

Table of Contents

Introduction 4

Chapter 1
Growing Up at Nishkwa-kwan-sing 7

Chapter 2
The Class Artist 12

Chapter 3
The Hayward Indian School
and a Long Hospital Stay 14

Chapter 4
A New Paint Box...................... 17

Chapter 5
Graphic Arts and Painting 20

Chapter 6
From Chippewa City to New York City... 22

Chapter 7
Beyond the Horizon 25

Chapter 8
An Artist Who Happens to Be Ojibwe ... 29

Chapter 9
Professor George Morrison............. 33

Chapter 10
Paintings in Wood..................... 36

Chapter 11
Land, Rocks, and Trees 41

Historical Context 46
Timeline 47
Glossary 50
Source Notes........... 51
Extend Your Learning 52

Introduction

Storytelling, a traditional tool of many Indigenous peoples, is alive and well among Native Americans of many nations. The authors, illustrators, and editors of this series, who are all Dakota or Ojibwe, continue their cultural traditions in creating these books and telling stories of leaders, athletes, teachers, and artists.

This series of books is by, for, and about Dakota and Anishinaabe (Ojibwe) and other Indigenous peoples. In portraying our histories, knowledge ways, culture keepers, and beloved figures, these biographies help Dakota, Anishinaabe, and other Native American children imagine their own potential for full futures.

We prefer to be called by our tribal names (Dakota, Ojibwe, or Anishinabe) or "Native American" or "Indigenous." We use "Indian" in numerous contexts today, such as the "National Museum of the American Indian." In this series, you will see the use of the term "Indian" in historical context, and not as a derogatory name.

We hope readers will consider how the facts of social barriers based on race, culture, education, and class are part of the life stories in these books. History, especially the impacts of treaties, underlies these stories as well. The legacy of forced education in the English language by government and religious schools, poverty, and the disruption of family life are also themes. The Indigenous peoples featured in these narratives overcame such circumstances. Natural talent in art and sports, leadership skills, and Native American cultural strengths are also themes of their stories.

This series includes stories of historical figures who lived, worked, and broke barriers a hundred years ago, as well as the ongoing accomplishments of exceptional Ojibwe and Dakota people who became leaders, athletes, teachers, and artists, and whose life stories are meaningful today. Our hope is that you see yourselves in the extraordinary lives presented in these books.

—Gwen N. Westerman and Heid E. Erdrich, series editors, May 2024

George Morrison
Gwe-ki-ge-nah-gah-boo
Wah-wah-ta-ga-nah-gah-boo

Chapter 1
Growing Up at Nishkwa-kwan-sing

Born in 1919, George Morrison grew up in Nishkwa-kwan-sing, an Ojibwe village on the edge of a vast forest on Gichigami (Lake Superior). He recalled a happy childhood there. He walked often on the shore, footsteps crunching on beach gravel, hearing hungry seagulls chasing fishing boats.

One day when he was close to the water's edge, George noticed a feather and carefully picked it up by the quill. It was one-third white and two-thirds black, which told George it was dropped by Migizi—the eagle. George turned the feather back and forth in the air, lining up the color white with the water and

the color black with the sky, nearly matching the lines of the feather to the line of the horizon—that place at the edge of the world where the water and sky meet. Finding an eagle feather was a gift from the Creator. George's grandmother taught him to leave a gift of asemaa, tobacco medicine, before taking anything from the lake or forest, but he had none, just water buckets to fill for his family. George put the feather in the water and watched it float toward the mysterious worlds beyond the horizon.

Later in life, George was known by two Ojibwe names: Gwe-ki-ge-nah-gah-boo, "Turning the Feather Around," and Wah-wah-ta-ga-nah-gah-boo, "Standing in the Northern Lights." Both names help describe George's personality and the artist he grew up to be.

The Morrison family lived in a four-room log house surrounded by great natural beauty near the

The Five Clans

Bear, loon, crane, marten, and sturgeon are five beings that live in the woods and waters of Minnesota. They are also the original five clans of the Ojibwe Nation. The people of Nishkwa-kwan-sing connected to one another as families and as clan members, all a part of the mighty Anishinaabe Nation—the original people of the Great Lakes. Anishinaabe homelands are in Minnesota, North Dakota, Wisconsin, Michigan, and Ontario, Canada.

village of Nishkwa-kwan-sing, also called Chippewa City. Chippewa was a name non-Native people called the Ojibwe. The village didn't have the bright lights, traffic, and roads that are in cities today. Instead, people walked on trails and used oil lamps for light. In winter, families often hitched dog teams to sleds to go find firewood or hunt for food. A family without dogs would use bent wood snowshoes laced with strips of deer or moose hide to walk in deep snow. The snow is often very deep in the land of the Ojibwe.

George's father, James Morrison, was born in 1890. He was Ojibwe and Scottish. George's mother, Barbara Mesaba, was Ojibwe and French from Canada. They had eleven children.

George's family lived close to his relatives in Chippewa City. His father and uncle Joe worked as trappers, loading up packs and walking 23 miles (37 km) through the forest to their winter camp on the South Brule River. By trapping animals for fur, Ojibwe people could make enough money to buy what they needed all year.

Many Ojibwe families relied on harvesting wild foods because they had little money for grocery stores. Most families fished for trout and herring, which they also traded or sold in Grand Marais, Minnesota. George and his siblings picked wild berries to sell to restaurants for ten cents a quart. George remembers picking blueberries, raspberries, strawberries, gooseberries, and chokecherries to make jams and jellies.

Plentiful wild rabbits, deer, grouse, and moose provided meat. People also made a type of bread called bannock. When George grew up, he learned about foods from all over the world. He always enjoyed cooking big meals and remembering the foods he ate as a child in Nishkwa-kwan-sing.

Chapter 2
The Class Artist

> I believe in going back to the magic of the earth and the lake, the sky and the universe. That kind of magic. I believe in that kind of religion. A religion of the rocks, the lake, the water, the sky.
>
> –George Morrison

George and his family attended St. Francis Xavier Catholic Church almost every Sunday. If the traveling priest was unavailable, George's grandfather James Morrison Sr. sometimes led the prayers. George and his family also believed in the traditional Ojibwe ways of his grandma Morrison and their ancestors. George recalled that his grandma built Ojibwe-style wigwams—portable tree bark homes that can be packed and carried from place to place—and always carried asemaa in a pouch.

He considered her a mashkiki-wikwe—a medicine woman who understood how to help people using medicines she grew and picked in the woods.

George's family did not have money for toys and art supplies, so he and his siblings made things from discarded objects. An old hand cart became a sled or a toy wagon, and a wooden box became a spinning top or a toy boat. George spent hours drawing on any scrap of paper he could find. He especially liked drawing objects he found and copying pictures from books or magazines. He taught himself about colors, shapes, lines, perspective, and shading. To learn how things were made, George used his creative skills to deconstruct and reconstruct objects.

Chippewa City children attended school in Grand Marais, 1 mile (1.6 km) away on the "Old Road" that followed the shore of Lake Superior. George spoke only Ojibwemowin until he went to school, where Ojibwe children learned to read, write, and speak English. George used his artistic talent right away. He said, "I used to make illustrations for some of the town kids, for their schoolwork. Then they would give me a swap—a jackknife or something."

Chapter 3
The Hayward Indian School and a Long Hospital Stay

Life was hard for the Morrison family and others on the North Shore of Lake Superior, especially for big families with many children and little money. The United States was struggling through the Great Depression. Many adults lost their jobs and families suffered.

George's family decided that George and two of his brothers would attend Hayward Indian School in Wisconsin. They joined about 150 students that lived at the boarding school while attending classes. George's older sister, Mary, stayed at home to help care for the younger children.

George and his brothers stayed at the school for the whole nine-month period. With no car and no money to buy bus tickets, his parents were unable to visit. Making art helped keep George focused and kept him and his brothers from feeling lonesome. At Hayward, George was again the class artist and was chosen to create posters for the school.

The Morrison brothers went home in the summer but returned to boarding school in the fall. During his second year at Hayward, George's hip started to hurt. When he was unable to walk, he was sent first to a hospital for Native American patients in Onigum, Minnesota, then to Gillette Children's hospital in St. Paul, Minnesota. There, children could get care from doctors who study muscles and bones. A disease called tuberculosis was affecting George's hip, and he needed surgery. George woke up after the operation wearing casts on each leg.

He stayed in the hospital for eight months. Although he was stuck in bed, George was still able to see the bright side of the hospital. He worked on art projects and read books on many subjects.

The hospital invited circus performers, movie stars, and even the famous boxer Jack Dempsey to visit the children. The people caring for George would wheel his hospital bed into the auditorium whenever there was a special guest. George was getting better and was learning more about the world and about himself. He would use this knowledge throughout his life.

Chapter 4
A New Paint Box

George returned home to Nishkwa-kwan-sing when he had healed enough to walk. He went back to school in Grand Marais. Other students there were interested in playing sports, but as George put it, "Having a lame leg made me very shy. Otherwise, I might have been more outgoing, playing ball, being part of a team."

George continued to swap pieces of artwork with other students, trading for art supplies or carving knives. He created mini drums, toy bows and arrows, or kid-sized tomahawks to sell in the stores in Grand Marais. He crafted colorfully decorated wooden birdhouses and tie racks that tourists bought as souvenirs. George also made money fixing worn-out library books, a job that paid six dollars a month.

As a teenager, George developed an interest in music. He spent some of his money on a guitar, a banjo, and a mandolin, and he learned to play each. Sometimes George would play music with a group of friends and family for dances at Anakwad Hall in Chippewa City.

As he got older, George's interest in reading deepened. He received an A+ grade in a high-school class called Manual Training, where he learned about technical drawing, furniture design, and illustration. At seventeen, George worked at a Civilian Conservation Corps camp on the Grand Portage Reservation. He worked in the kitchen and the woods along with other young Ojibwe men.

George Morrison (*right*) in 1938 with the chair he designed in a class at Grand Marais High School

In 1938, George graduated from Grand Marais High School. He was the first person in his family to graduate from high school. His English teacher and neighbor took an interest in George's artistic talents and encouraged him to attend the Minneapolis School of Art, now known as the Minneapolis College of Art and Design. Students at this college learned painting, graphics, drawing, sculpture, and design.

Chapter 5
Graphic Arts and Painting

At art school, Morrison studied graphic arts. He drew the human body on paper and painted portraits of people using a palette knife instead of a paintbrush. He read about art history and modern artists and visited museums to see work by other artists.

In 1939, the Minneapolis Institute of Art, which was near Morrison's college, exhibited artwork by Spanish artist Pablo Picasso. Picasso invented an artistic form called Cubism, a way of deconstructing and then reconstructing subjects in paintings. Imagine all six sides of a box being flattened out and drawn in a single layer—this is Cubism. The subject of a Cubist work of art could be anything: a person, an animal, a landscape, or other objects.

Morrison was inspired by Picasso's Cubist work and decided to switch from studying graphic arts to studying painting. As a self-taught artist, the idea of deconstructing and then reconstructing things in a new way helped Morrison explore ways of seeing the world.

Morrison often thought of his home on Lake Superior. His mother could not write in English, like many Ojibwe speakers of the time. But his older sister helped his mother write to him. After his first year at college, Morrison returned to Chippewa City to help his family while he created new paintings and drawings.

Chapter 6
From Chippewa City to New York City

In 1942, Morrison got a full scholarship from the Woman's Club of Minneapolis to pay for his second year of art school. He returned to Minneapolis, but he was still having health problems. His left leg didn't grow as fast as his right leg. Morrison had to have another surgery, which made him miss his second year of college.

Morrison returned home with his box of paints. There were only four or five families left in Nishkwakwan-sing. Most people had moved away. While his leg got better, Morrison stayed with his brother and family in a little cabin under the fire tower

Mount Maude by George Morrison, 1942

at the base of Mount Maud on the Grand Portage Reservation. He kept painting, experimenting with art forms, and capturing the beauty of the lake, the trees, and the rocky hills all around him.

When he returned to the Minneapolis School of Art that fall, Morrison had new ideas to explore. His teachers connected him with new ways to express his view of the world through art. Morrison jumped into the creative world with both feet. He experimented and enjoyed other forms of art, such as ballet, theater, and classical music.

Morrison focused on art school, dreaming of continuing his studies in New York City. When he graduated from the Minneapolis School of Art in 1943, Morrison was awarded a full scholarship to the Art Students League, a top school for artists in New York. His mother made the trip from Chippewa City to Minneapolis to celebrate his graduation.

That fall, Morrison left his childhood home at Nishkwa-kwan-sing and bought a one-way train ticket to New York City. He took one suitcase and the paint box he bought when he first went to art school.

World War II (1939–1945)

In 1942, the United States sent soldiers to Europe to fight Nazi Germany. War affected every city and town. Even Chippewa City and Grand Portage Reservation lost soldiers to battles far across the ocean. Two of Morrison's friends from high school died fighting in World War II. Due to his physical disability, Morrison could not serve in the military.

Chapter 7
Beyond the Horizon

When Morrison arrived in New York City, the world was still at war. New York's lights were dimmed at night to make it harder for enemy airplanes to find their targets. When the war ended, Morrison remembered New York City as "a magical city—bridges and all of Manhattan lit up."

Morrison's new school, the Art Students League, was founded in 1875. Its artists were from all over the world, and Morrison fit in nicely. He moved into an apartment in Greenwich Village—a neighborhood full of artists, writers, and creative people. Morrison described this period as a time of artistic freedom; he and his fellow artists were free to create what they wanted.

   Morrison painted every day and took his sketchbook when he explored the city. He sketched people on the subway, drew life on the city streets, and learned the differences between modern styles of painting. One of Morrison's teachers was Morris Kantor, an American painter who worked in Cubism, the style of the Picasso paintings Morrison admired. Morrison often ate dinner with his teacher and other students, trying food from countries such as Greece, Italy, and China.

   As Morrison's world got bigger, his own artwork began to expand and change. He learned of Expressionism. He experimented with this style

Art Styles

In addition to Cubism, Morrison used many art styles in his works. Expressionism is a style of art that was popular in the 1930s and 1940s. It uses distorted or exaggerated shapes, colors, and textures to show an artist's thoughts or emotions about a subject. It broke away from Realism, a traditional style of art that depicts everyday life in a real or natural way. Abstract art uses lines, colors, shapes, and forms to represent a reality, while still life is a genre of art of nonliving objects. Surrealism is art that is created from the imagination, or sometimes it can emerge out of layers of paint on canvas.

and added elements of Cubism to his work. He did very well at art college, but he missed his family and Lake Superior.

When Morrison returned home for the summer in 1944, many Ojibwe had left to work in big cities. His parents had separated, and Morrison's father had moved to Duluth, Minnesota. Although Chippewa City was very different from when Morrison was a boy, he kept making art there as he always had. He submitted an original portrait to the Minnesota State Fair and won third place.

Back in New York that fall, Morrison was included in student art shows at the Art Students League. He also sold paintings there. He remembered selling small paintings for ten dollars. "Of course, ten bucks was more than it is today," Morrison said. "A good ten bucks." Since painting did not pay much, Morrison had other jobs in New York: building picture frames, carpentry, and painting clothing buttons at a factory.

Instead of returning home in 1945, Morrison traveled with friends to Provincetown, Massachusetts, a fishing village at the tip of Cape Cod. It reminded him of his home in Minnesota. The Atlantic Ocean and Lake Superior were both "big waters" to Morrison. His connection to Gichigami, "big water" in Ojibwe, was always important to who he was as a person and an artist. Morrison always searched for what could be discovered beyond the horizon.

Chapter 8
An Artist Who Happens to Be Ojibwe

As the war ended, Morrison and other artists formed a collective called the Pyramid Group. They worked together on group exhibitions at small galleries, which led to showings at bigger galleries. In 1946, Morrison's art was on view at the Whitney Museum of American Art in New York. He won the fourth-place cash prize at Grand Central Art Galleries with his painting *Still Life*.

Soon after, Morrison was invited to teach at the Cape Ann Art School. He was making good money as an artist, but Morrison still liked to trade his art for other items. He traded a watercolor painting for a coal-black poodle he named Kobi, who became his constant companion.

In the late 1940s, Morrison played with different textures and painted on wood. He explored the Abstract style of painting and drawing and created still lifes and landscapes with driftwood, rocks, and other things he found on the beaches of Cape Cod. He began to explore what he called an imaginary "vast horizon." He used Expressionist and Cubist techniques, along with a shifting horizon line, to tell a deeper story about the fish, trees, and objects he put on canvas.

Morrison met his first wife, Ada Reed, in Provincetown. They married in 1948. Soon after, his first solo show in Manhattan was reviewed by several art critics. The critic from *The Sun* (New York City) found a connection to Morrison's Ojibwe ancestry in the way that he painted. Morrison's Ojibwe background shone through his modern style and was recognized by a growing audience of admirers.

In November 1949, Morrison's father passed away. Morrison returned to Chippewa City for the funeral at St. Francis Xavier, the church that Morrison went to as a child and where his great-grandfather had rung the bell every Sunday. Morrison's Uncle

Joe died a few months later. Both are buried in the Chippewa City cemetery.

In 1952, Morrison was awarded a Fulbright Scholarship to study in France. He, Ada, and Kobi the poodle boarded the *Queen Mary* and sailed to Paris. They lived in Paris for three months while Morrison studied at the École des Beaux-Arts. They traveled to other parts of France and Spain, and Morrison's work caught the eye of French art critics.

One year later, Morrison and Ada decided to move back to Minnesota. They rented a house in Duluth, where Morrison's mother lived. He continued to paint and liked to work at night in his home studio.

A few of Morrison's paintings were included in a show of Native American artists in San Francisco, California. It was in that exhibit that art critics first connected Morrison's work with the art of other modern, Native American artists such as Oscar Howe, a Dakota artist from South Dakota. Morrison and Howe would later become friends, and they would both work with Native American art students as teachers and mentors.

By 1954, Morrison and Ada divorced. He and Kobi were back in New York City where Abstract Expressionism was the artistic trend on view in galleries and museums. This modern art style began in New York with painters such as Jackson Pollock, Willem de Kooning, and Joan Miró. Morrison's work in the 1950s combined elements of Abstraction, Expressionism, Cubism, and Surrealism.

His work was being recognized by large galleries. Morrison submitted paintings for a Native American artist exhibit at the Philbrook Museum of Art in Tulsa, Oklahoma. To Morrison's surprise, his work was turned down. The curator said it "wasn't Indian enough" to be included. Even though Morrison was born into an Ojibwe family and raised in an Ojibwe community, his style and artistic expression did not fit the 1950s definition of Native American art.

Being rejected by the Philbrook Museum of Art helped Morrison define himself as an artist on his own terms. After that, when asked if he was a Native American artist Morrison often replied, "I never played the role of being an Indian artist. I always just stated the fact that I was a painter, and I happened to be Indian."

Chapter 9
Professor George Morrison

In the late 1950s, Morrison's distinct paintings and drawings began to gain value. Art collectors from all over the world bought his work. He was becoming famous. In 1958, the town of Grand Marais honored Morrison with the Distinguished Citizen Award. His mother and several of his siblings attended the celebration dinner.

Morrison was invited to return to the Minneapolis School of Art as a visiting artist and teacher. He taught there for one month and then accepted an invitation to teach at the Dayton Art Institute in Dayton, Ohio. There, Morrison met Hazel Belvo, a painter interested in modern, new ideas. As Hazel explained, "When I visited his studio after the first class, he was working on a large canvas, painting with pure pigment right out of the tube . . . it was a wonderful painting . . . I felt as though we'd known each other forever." They were married in 1960, and one year later, their son, Briand, was born.

Even though Morrison's art was popular, he needed another job to support his family. With Hazel's help, they listed his artistic accomplishments and sent his work history to more than one hundred art schools and colleges. Morrison was hired to teach at top art schools including Iowa State, Pennsylvania State, and Cornell University.

Morrison, his wife, Hazel, and their son, Briand, circa 1978

In 1963, the Rhode Island School of Design hired Morrison as an assistant professor. He and his family moved to an old farmhouse first, then near the waterfront. Morrison's art became inspired by the rock formations he knew so well as a child. His images on canvas used many, many layers of paint and textures. Sometimes the paint built up to 0.25 inches (0.6 cm) thick.

His mother passed away in 1969, and Morrison traveled to Duluth for her funeral. That same year, Morrison received an honorary master's degree from the Minneapolis School of Art.

Chapter 10
Paintings in Wood

Morrison's family spent summers walking on the beach in Provincetown, Massachusetts, where Hazel's older sons would join them. Morrison remembered one time, "we found driftwood from all over the world—the South Seas, the Caribbean, the North Atlantic. It all washed up on this tip of Cape Cod.... There was an interesting history in those pieces—who had touched them, where they had come from. I collected them and the kids collected them."

Morrison began to create wood collages—making beautiful, new art from bits and pieces of discarded things, like he had done as a boy growing up in Chippewa City. "Paintings in wood—that's how I see them.... There's a horizon line in each one, about a quarter of the way from the top." Some of Morrison's wood collages included hundreds of pieces of wood and objects that Morrison and others had found or collected over the years.

In 1970, Morrison began teaching in the new Department of American Indian Studies at the University of Minnesota in Minneapolis. Even though the family was settled in Rhode Island, Morrison said he felt he needed to come back to an Ojibwe connection, to Minnesota, and to his family. The family bought an old church in St. Paul and renovated it to fit two artist studios and bedrooms.

Morrison became active in the large Native American community in Minneapolis and St. Paul. The 1970s were a time of change, with the formation of the American Indian Movement (AIM) and growing awareness about Native American culture, history, and arts.

As he did all throughout his life, Morrison added more books to his personal library and continued

Morrison in his home studio in St. Paul, Minnesota, in the 1970s

to study and research topics that interested him. He would then bring those topics into the courses he was teaching at the university. Some of Morrison's students would also become well-known artists, including Frank Bigbear Jr. and sculptor Kent Smith.

Morrison carried his experiments in wood collage along with him from the Atlantic Coast. These large-scale works of art were related to the Abstract style but were based on landscape, which included the sea and sky. The Minneapolis Institute of Art bought the first one he made. That wood collage, *Landscape*, is still in the museum's collection.

Patricia Hobot, Lakota gallery director at the Minneapolis American Indian Center in the 1970s, described Morrison's artwork as embodying Native American values and showing how the individual is

Untitled wood relief by George Morrison, 1975

expected to fit into the whole. Through his careful arrangement of color and pieces of wood, Morrison was able to connect others to his Ojibwe culture while honoring the place where he was from. "The basis of all art is nature," he said. "It creeps in even to abstract art. The look of the North Shore was subconsciously in my psyche, prompting some of my images."

In 1974, the Walker Art Center exhibited forty-five of Morrison's large pen-and-ink drawings. Using intricately drawn, straight lines on paper, the drawings stayed true to Morrison's unique style—mixing in elements of Cubism, Abstraction, and Surrealism. At the same time, Morrison was invited to create an art piece for the outside of the Minneapolis American Indian Center that the city of Minneapolis was building. Inspired by the symbolism of feathers to Indigenous peoples, the wood collage gives the feeling of turning a feather around. The mural was dedicated in 1975 and later cleaned and restored when the Minneapolis American Indian Center was remodeled in 2024. Morrison also created wood collages for the Daybreak Star Indian Cultural Center in Seattle and for the University of Minnesota Law School.

Morrison's work on these wooden murals inspired him to create three-dimensional sculptures. Flat drawings and paintings are two-dimensional, having just two measurements—height and width. Sculptures have three dimensions—height, width, and depth. Totems are important to many Native American cultures, and Morrison's tall, slender monuments, made of exotic wood or painted earthy red, are his own, unique version of the traditional totem pole.

Chapter 11
Land, Rocks, and Trees

One thing that made me come back is the land, I feel a reverence for the land and the lake. You come back to your own environment and how you grew up.

–George Morrison

As a professor and working artist, Morrison was very busy. He received a lot of invitations from all over the world to teach or present his work, including a trip to Havana, Cuba, as part of a cultural exchange. But when Morrison turned sixty years old, he fell ill and had to have surgery. According to Hazel, that's when Morrison started talking about returning to the North Shore, where he was born.

By the time Morrison decided to return home, Chippewa City no longer existed as a village. But as a Grand Portage tribal member, Morrison was able to build his studio within the borders of the reservation. His ancestors, like the ancestors of other Grand Portage families, reserved land on the reservation under the US government's General Allotment Act of 1887. But in most cases, that land was deep in the woods with no roads, so most families sold it to timber companies. Morrison and Hazel chose land on Lake Superior that they called Red Rock. Though it was about 35 miles (56 km) east of Chippewa City, Red Rock had a clear view of the horizon.

After Morrison retired from the University of Minnesota in 1983, he focused on building a house and studio in Grand Portage because even though he was retiring from teaching, he would never retire from creating art. In 1984, Morrison got sick and needed long-term medical care. He and Hazel traveled between Grand Portage and Minneapolis for the next two years. Morrison worried that he would run out of time to explore new ideas in sculpture and drawings.

Walter Caribou, one of his grandmother's Caribou relatives, was a leader and mashkikiiwinini—a spiritual guide and medicine man for Grand Portage. Morrison asked Caribou for guidance, and Caribou held a healing ceremony, giving Morrison two spirit names that came to Caribou in dreams. The two names, Wah-wah-ta-ga-nah-gah-boo, "Standing in the Northern Lights," and Gwe-ki-ge-nah-gah-boo, "Turning the Feather Around," were very important to Morrison and helped guide him through the rest of his life. Along with the names, Caribou gave Morrison two feathers, which he treasured.

Despite being ill, Morrison continued to paint, working on small canvases mounted to blocks of wood, using every color to capture the ever-changing moods of Gichigami. "The phenomenon of the clouds and other images from nature—pebbles or rocks or trees on the beach—all come right in these windows," Morrison said. Morrison's *Horizon* series was featured in solo shows at the Tweed Museum of Art in Duluth and the Minnesota Museum of American Art in St. Paul. Morrison said that the naming ceremony made him stronger and that his life was coming full circle. "As a boy, I had carried water up from the lake for our family to drink," he reflected. "Now I was living much of the time by the lake again."

In May of 1990, a retrospective of Morrison's work opened at the Minnesota Museum of American Art. The show traveled to the Tweed Museum of Art and then to the Plains Art Museum in Fargo, North Dakota. It included paintings, drawings, totems, collages, and Churingas—carved, rounded-edged, wooden sculptures designed by Morrison in the late 1980s. He explained that "I wanted to have a big show that would pull my work together." His wishes for a big show had come true.

Morrison shared the story of his life in a book, *Turning the Feather Around: My Life in Art.* At the end of the book, Morrison talks about his lifelong relationship to the horizon, whether in Chippewa City, Provincetown, or Grand Portage: "From the horizon you go beyond the edge of the world to the sky and, beyond that, to the unknown. I always imagine, in a certain surrealist way, that I am there. I like to imagine it is real."

In 1997, Morrison's *Red Totem* was installed in the Jacqueline Kennedy Sculpture Garden at the White House as part of the exhibition *Honoring Native America*. Morrison attended the opening ceremony, where he met First Lady Hillary Clinton.

He continued to draw, paint, sculpt, and imagine new worlds beyond the horizon until his death in 2000. He never stopped creating art or being curious about the world. His memorial was held at the St. Francis Xavier Church in Chippewa City, which was opened especially for the service.

Morrison's work and legacy continue to be honored in galleries and collections across the globe. In 2020, Morrison became the first Native American artist included in the New York School collection of the National Gallery of Art in Washington, DC. In 2024, the University of Minnesota opened the George Morrison Center for Indigenous Arts to support the creation, presentation, and interpretation of Indigenous art in all its forms.

Historical Context

The Dakota and Ojibwe people have histories as rich and full of struggle as the US or other countries. This timeline presents important events in one place as a reminder that no one human history is more important than another, but history often makes it look that way. This timeline also provides context from the Dakota and Ojibwe histories. You can use it to respond to the book by comparing the timelines of each person featured in this series to the events listed here.

Beyond memory, this place called Mni Sota Makoce, or Minnesota, is where the people became Dakota. They traveled as far north as Hudson's Bay in Canada, as far west as the Rocky Mountains, south to trade with the Pueblos, and to the southeast past the trading city of Cahokia to the southeastern part of what became the United States.

During this same time, Anishinaabeg, the larger group that includes Ojibwe people, lived far to the east of Minnesota, near the Atlantic Ocean. A series of prophecies, or visions of their future, set the Ojibwe off on their five-hundred-year journey to find a new home in "a land where food grows on water," (meaning manoomin, wild rice) along the Great Lakes and eventually in Minnesota.

Timeline

900–1400	The Dakota live, as they have always, in what will become Minnesota; ancestors of other Indigenous groups, including the Ojibwe, begin migrating west.
1540–1622	Spanish and French explorers map the Mississippi River and Dakota village sites and make contact with the Ojibwe at Lake Superior.
1730–1850	Ojibwe and Dakota fight over Dakota territories; battles end with their peace agreement in 1870, which remains unbroken.
1776–1783	The American Revolution is fought.
1805	The Dakota agree to sell land to the US government, but the US government never pays.
1819	Fort St. Anthony, renamed Fort Snelling in 1825, is built at Bdote (meeting place of rivers in present-day St. Paul, Minnesota).
1825	The Dakota and Ojibwe lose land in the Prairie du Chien treaty.
1830	Congress passes the Indian Removal Act, forcing all Native Americans to move west of the Mississippi River.
1837–1850s	Treaties force the Dakota and Ojibwe onto reservations, and they lose hundreds of millions of acres of homeland.
1849–1857	Minnesota Territory is established, and American settlers encroach on Dakota lands.

1858	Minnesota becomes a state.
1861–1865	The American Civil War is fought.
1862	War between the Dakota and the US begins in August and ends in September.
1863	The US repeals treaties, and almost all Dakota are removed from Minnesota.
1880s	The Dakota people begin to return to their communities in Minnesota.
1919	**George Morrison is born.**
1924	Congress passes the Indian Citizenship Act, granting citizenship to all Native Americans.
1943	**Morrison graduates from the Minneapolis School of Art and begins studying at the Arts Students League in New York City.**
1948	**Morrison's first solo art show takes place in Manhattan, New York City.**
1952	**Morrison is awarded a Fulbright Scholarship to study in France.**
1953	The US makes laws to end the legal status of tribes as nations during the years known as the Termination era.
1956	The Indian Relocation Act passes to move Native Americans off reservations to cities.

1978   The American Indian Religious Freedom Act ends the outlaw of a tribe's religious and cultural practices.

1997   **Morrison's *Red Totem* is installed in the Jacqueline Kennedy Sculpture Garden at the White House.**

2000   Morrison dies.

2024   The University of Minnesota opens the George Morrison Center for Indigenous Arts.

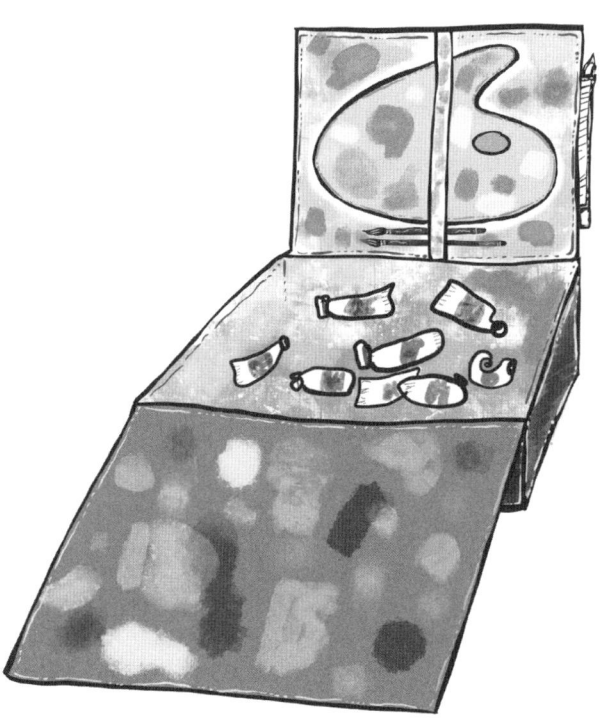

Glossary

art critic: a professional who analyzes and interprets art

asemaa: tobacco; one of the four sacred medicines in Ojibwe culture

curator: the person in charge of a museum or art collection

deconstruct: to take apart

Great Depression: an economic crisis from 1929 to 1941 in the US where many people lost their jobs and banks closed, leaving people poor and homeless

mural: a work of art such as a painting that is made as part of a structure such as a wall or ceiling

Ojibwemowin: also known as Anishinaabemowin, the Indigenous language of the Ojibwe people

palette knife: a thin steel blade with a handle used for mixing colors

reconstruct: to put together again

scholarship: money given to students to help pay for their education

tuberculosis: also known as TB, a bacterial disease that usually affects the lungs but can also affect bones and other parts of the body

Source Notes

12 George Morrison and Margot Fortunato Galt, *Turning the Feather Around: My Life in Art* (Minnesota Historical Society Press, 1998), 29.

13 Morrison and Galt, 37.

17 Morrison and Galt, 43.

25 Morrison and Galt, 59.

28 Morrison and Galt, 66.

32 Charleen Touchette, "George Morrison (1919–2000): Standing on the 'Edge of the World,'" *American Indian Art Magazine*, Winter 2001, 76.

32 Morrison and Galt, 71.

34 Morrison and Galt, 113.

36 Morrison and Galt, 125.

36–37 Morrison and Galt, 128.

39 Morrison and Galt, 146.

41 "George Morrison," National Park Service, accessed January 27, 2025, https://www.nps.gov/articles/000/george-morrison.htm.

43 Morrison and Galt, 168.

44 Morrison and Galt, 172.

44 Morrison and Galt, 166.

44 Morrison and Galt, 192.

Extend Your Learning

IDEAS FOR WRITING AND DISCUSSION

- What moment in this story do you think you will most remember? Why?

- Who do you believe was most important to this person's success? Why?

- What do you think were the hardest moments for this person? Why?

- How do you think this person was able to overcome hardship in their life?

- What were the happiest moments in the story of this person's life?

- What moment in the story reminded you of something in your own life?

- Write your own short autobiography, the story of your life so far!

IDEAS FOR VISUAL PROJECTS

- Draw images for three or four moments that are not illustrated in this book.

- Draw a sketch of this person and include items they liked.

- Find images from American Indian Boarding Schools from the time this book covers.

- Find historic images to share of activities this book mentions. Are they different now?

- Find historic images to share of the reservations or places this book mentions.

- Make a map of tribal nations near where you live. Where are reservations located? What tribes live there? What else did you learn about these tribal nations?

- Create a bar graph, pie chart, or other infographic on one of these topics:

    1. How many Native Americans live in urban areas near you? Which US cities are home to the largest populations of Native Americans?
    2. How many Native American students are there in your school district? How many tribes are represented?
    3. Explore "Why Treaties Matter" and give a brief report about how treaties formed the reservations and the homelands of Dakota and Ojibwe peoples.

Resources for Visual Projects
American Indian Education: Teaching and Learning
https://education.mn.gov/MDE/dse/indian/teach/

Why Treaties Matter
https://treatiesmatter.org/exhibit/

IDEAS FOR FURTHER LEARNING
The Dakota and Ojibwe people continue to live in Minnesota and are part of all aspects of our society. While English is a shared language, many Dakota and Ojibwe people also study and speak Dakota and Anishinaabemowin, their Indigenous languages.

- Find unfamiliar words in this book and create a glossary or word list with definitions.

- Create a timeline for this person's life.

- Learn how to count to ten in Dakota or Ojibwe.

- Look up Ojibwe or Dakota words for baseball or ball games such as lacrosse.

- Learn about Dakota and Ojibwe sports and activities such as powwows.

- Make a list of four common traditions the Ojibwe and Dakota share.

Resources to Learn More

Historic Fort Snelling: Educator Resources
https://www.mnhs.org/fortsnelling/learn/educator-resources

Minnesota Historical Society: Beginning Dakota
http://beginningdakota.org

Minnesota Historical Society: Minnesota Territory
http://www.mnhs.org/talesoftheterritory

Minnesota Historical Society: Ojibwe Material Culture
http://www.mnhs.org/ojibwematerialculture

The Ojibwe People's Dictionary
https://ojibwe.lib.umn.edu

About the Author

Staci Lola Drouillard is a Grand Portage Band of Ojibwe direct descendant. She lives and works in her hometown of Kitchibitobig—Grand Marais, on Minnesota's North Shore of Lake Superior. Her first book, *Walking the Old Road: A People's History of Chippewa City and the Grand Marais Anishinaabe* (2019), won the Hamlin Garland Prize in Popular History and the Northeastern Minnesota Book Award for nonfiction and was a finalist for a Minnesota Book Award. Her second book, *Seven Aunts* (2022), won the 2023 Minnesota Book Award for Memoir and Creative Nonfiction and the Northeastern Minnesota Book Award and was a "Minnesota Reads" selection at the Library of Congress National Book Festival. *A Family Tree* (2024) is her first children's book and was illustrated by Kate Gardiner.

About the Illustrator

Tashia Hart is an author and illustrator; her works include *Native Love Jams* (2023), *The Good Berry Cookbook: Harvesting and Cooking Wild Rice and Other Wild Foods* (2021), *Gidjie and the Wolves* (2020), and *Girl Unreserved* (2015). She was assistant illustrator for *Gaa-pi-izhiwebak* (2021) and illustrator for *Gidjie and the Wolves* (2020). Her short works include recipes, essays, poetry, and short stories for various publications. In addition to this title, she has also illustrated several of the books in this series. She is a citizen of the Red Lake Nation and resides in Duluth, Minnesota.

About the Series Editors

Heid E. Erdrich is a member of the Ojibwe Nation enrolled at the Turtle Mountain Reservation in North Dakota. She grew up in Wahpeton, North Dakota. She is also German American and Metis from Canada. Erdrich has written several books of poetry and a cookbook focused on Indigenous foods. Along with being Anishinaabe/Ojibwe, Erdrich's extended family includes Dakota, Hidatsa, Somali American, German American, and immigrants from India. She loves the stories of how many kinds of people came to call one place home. Erdrich has lived in Minnesota for many years, raising her kids in Minneapolis, where they went to public schools.

Gwen N. Westerman is Dakota from the Sisseton Wahpeton Oyate and a citizen of the Cherokee Nation of Oklahoma. She grew up in Kansas among many different tribal nations. Today, she writes about Dakota history, and writes poetry in English and Dakota. Westerman's ancestors were teachers, leaders, and hard workers who were Dakota, Cherokee, Ojibwe, and Odawa along with a few French and Scottish traders. She lives in Minnesota, where her kids grew up playing ice hockey and soccer.